生命的意义

The Meaning of Life

布拉德里·特雷弗·格里夫　著

曹化银　译

中 信 出 版 社

辽宁教育出版社

图书在版编目（CIP）数据

生命的意义 / 格里夫著；曹化银译. –北京：中信出版社，2002.8
书名原文：The Meaning of Life
ISBN 7-80073-498-6

Ⅰ.生… Ⅱ.① 格… ② 曹… Ⅲ.人生观–通俗读物 Ⅳ.B821–49

中国版本图书馆CIP数据核字（2002）第054008号

生命的意义
SHENGMING DE YIYI

作　　者：布拉德里·特雷弗·格里夫

译　　者：曹化银

责任编辑：潘　岳　责任监制：朱　磊　王祖力

出 版 者：中信出版社　辽宁教育出版社

经 销 者：中信联合发行有限公司

承 印 者：东莞金杯印刷有限公司

开　　本：787mm×1092mm　1/24　印　张：5.75　字　数：40千字

版　　次：2002年8月第1版　印　次：2002年8月第1次印刷

京权图字：01-2002-3358

书　　号：ISBN 7-80073-498-6/B·8

定　　价：26.00 元

生命的意义

致　谢

　　在此，我再次向克里斯廷·希林和她在安德鲁斯—麦克米尔的全明星团队表示真诚的感谢。还有兰登书屋（澳大利亚）的无与伦比的简·帕尔弗里曼，还有我在BTG摄影室中长期忍受寂寞的伙伴们，是他们使这本优雅的小书成功面世。

　　摄影家，以及展示他们作品的神圣的图书馆，是真理和美丽的信鸽。我也感谢他们让我站到了天才的肩上。

　　如果认为没有阿尔伯特·J·朱克曼，我即便能够取得一些成就，也是非常愚蠢的。他是一个文学经纪人，燃起了至关重要的火花，照亮了我的事业之路。但是谁会想到，这样一个曾经向东方集团贩运软糖以支付大学学费的人会在我的生活中变得如此显要呢？尽管如此，就像在1938年，作为马戏团的魔术师，他与一只关节灵活的雪貂一起漫游撒哈拉以南的非洲地区，筹集到第一笔资金，启动了纽约作家书屋一样，正是他无拘无束的创造性和不屈不挠的韧性让我变得小有名气。

序　言

暂停！吁！马上停下来！在你开始阅读之前，有些事情你必须先弄明白。

Halt! Whoa! Stop right there!

Before you read any further there's something

you really should know.

你打开这本小书的时候，可能期望里面充满了答案，
但它（出乎意料，出乎意料！）实际上是一本有关各种问题的书。
You may have opened this little book expecting it to be filled with answers,
but (surprise, surprise!) it's actually a book about questions.

这可能不是你想听到的话。

This may not be what you wanted to hear.

大多数人不喜欢问题，他们喜欢得到答案。而且，如果不能开门见山、
轻轻松松地得到答案，他们的眼睛马上就会呆钝起来。

Most people don't like questions—they like answers. And if they don't get easy
answers straight away, their eyes immediately start to glaze over.

他们很快就会做起可爱的白日梦，梦见跳舞的蛋糕、唱歌的萝卜，
或者浸泡在充满香草蛋羹的浴盆里。

Pretty soon they're off in a lovely daydream about dancing cupcakes,
singing turnips, and soaking in a bathtub filled with warm vanilla custard.

所以——这一点非常重要——如果你想说：
"问题？呸呸呸。谁需要问题？"
So, and this is important, if you feel like saying,
"Questions? Pffffffffff. Who needs them?"

那么，这是你把这本书抛到一旁、悠闲地去看重播的
《吉利根岛》的最后机会。我再说一遍，**这是你的最后机会。**

then this is your last chance to throw this book away and wander off to watch
reruns of Gilligan's Island. I repeat, this is your last chance.

生命的意义

不管怎么看，生命总是很奇特。

No matter how you look at it, life is strange.

非常奇特。

Very strange.

例如，我们都是由极其相同的物质组成的，是整个宇宙中最聪明、
最有创造力、最高贵的生命形式。这是一个不争的事实。

For example, it's an indisputable fact that we are all made of the precise same substance
as the most intelligent, creative, magnificent life-forms in the entire universe.

而且，构成我们的原子物质，与构成这个星球上最雄伟的山峰、
银河系中最明亮的星辰的物质完全相同。

Furthermore, we are composed of the exact same atomic matter as the mightiest
mountains on this planet and the brightest stars in the galaxy.

当然，土豆、蜗牛和肉肠也是如此——也许，这就是生命如此莫名其妙的原因。

Of course, this is also true for potatoes, snails, and meatloaf—perhaps that's
why there's so much about life that doesn't make a great deal of sense.

首先想一想，我们为什么会对巨大的物体和成就刮目相看、情有独钟？

For starters, why are we so overly impressed by and obsessed

with objects and achievements of immense scale,

而实际上，正是一个个细小的事物聚沙成塔，才造就了桩桩大事。

when it is actually the tiny little things that,

when put together, make big things possible?

我们为什么想方设法营造自己的小世界，结果产生错觉，

认为自己完全掌控了整个生命的存在？

Why do we try to create our own little worlds so we have the illusion of

being completely in control of our entire existence,

而我们千真万确地知道，事实并非如此。

when we know with absolute certainty

that we are not?

我们为什么一味追求个性，认为这是生命的本质，

Why do we go on and on about individuality

being the very essence of who we are,

继而又大言不惭地承认，几乎在生命的每一个方面，我们都存在共性呢？

and then accept a degrading level of conformity

in virtually every facet of our lives?

为什么孩子相信神话，而"大人"不相信呢？

Why do children believe in fairies,

but "grown-ups" don't?

为什么我们对分歧毫不让步，而事实上，
正是彼此间的差异才使生命如此有趣？

And why do we get so hung up on what we don't agree on,
when in fact it's our differences that make life interesting?

毕竟，总有一半世界是大头朝下的，所以完全没有理由要求我们事事意见相同。

After all, half the world is upside down, so there's absolutely no reason
why we would all agree on everything.

甚至像"不要张着嘴咀嚼"这样基本而深奥的道理，
也并不像你想像的那样广为接受。

Even something as basic and profound as "Don't chew with your mouth open"

is not as widely accepted as you might think.

怒火中烧时，我们为什么选择争吵和打斗，

Why is it that when passions are inflamed

we choose to argue and fight,

而实际上，跳一曲恰恰舞危险更小、更有情趣、更能化解紧张局面？
when dancing the cha-cha is less injurious, far more enjoyable,
and equally effective in resolving the tension?

作为同一物种，为什么我们感觉这样亲近，

And why do we feel drawn together as a species,

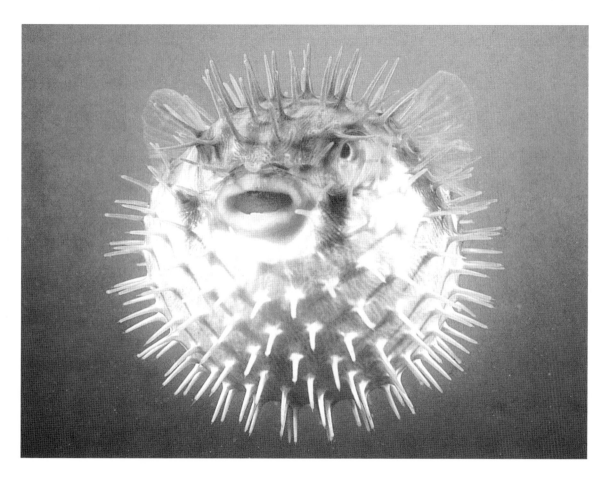

而为什么我们又总是披上自卫的外衣，掩饰内心深处的情感和信念，
使我们永远无法真正相互接近？

yet we steadily build up defensive barriers around our innermost feelings and
beliefs so we can never be truly close to anyone?

也许，生活并非总像表面上看起来的那样，所以才会出现困惑。

Perhaps the confusion arises because life

is not always what it seems.

作为一个物种，我们迷恋肤浅的外表。

As a species, we are obsessed with
superficial appearance.

我们都戴着有色眼镜，所以大多数人只看到自己想看到的东西。
最终睁开眼睛时，你可能会大为震惊，没想到为了满足个人的小算盘，
自己竟会这样模糊地看世界。

We all have filters on, so we mostly see only what we want to see.
When you finally open your eyes, you may be shocked at the obscured
way you have been viewing the world to suit your own little plans.

摘掉有色眼镜，你可以更真切地发现自我，询问有关宇宙以及你在其中的位置这类客观问题。换句话说，探究生命的意义。

With those filters removed, you can take a closer look into yourself and
ask objective questions about the universe and your place in it.
In other words, investigate the meaning of life.

那么生命的意义何在？嗯，你经常听人们说"生命是一段旅程"，
但确切地说，这段旅程的目的地是哪儿？

So what is life all about? Well, you often hear that "life is a journey,"
but a journey to where, exactly?

有些人说，生命的意义在于获取知识。如果是这样，
那么为什么聪明人总打扮得这样糟糕?

Some people say that life is all about acquiring knowledge. If that's true,

then why do smart people always dress so badly?

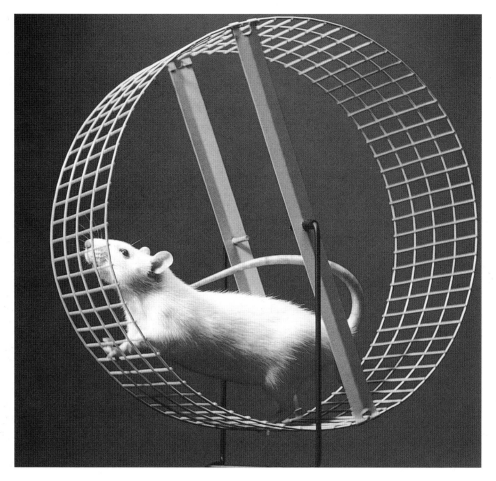

也有人说，生命根本没有目的，
生命就是"存在"。哇，简直太"深刻"了！
There are those who say that life has no purpose;
it just "is." Whoa, that's just so "deep!"

还有人说，我们来到世上，就是为了组建一个家庭。毕竟，
繁衍后代的迫切需要已经深深地印在了每个物种的基因图谱中。

Then there are people who say that we're simply here to have a family. After all,
the desperate need to replace ourselves is etched into the genetic map of every living thing.

但是，这意味着我们的整个存在都是由原始的性冲动驱使的。好吧，也许一个漫长的周末可以这样，但是整个生命历程呢？我不这样认为。

However, this means that our entire existence is driven by our primitive sexual urges. Okay, sure, a long weekend maybe, but our entire existence? I don't think so.

事实上，靠近一点儿，让我告诉你一个小秘密……

In fact, come a tiny bit closer and I'll let you in

on a little secret . . .

所有这些想法听起来都愚蠢无比!!!
ALL THESE IDEAS SOUND
COMPLETELY STUPID!!!

在无数广为流行的生命理论中，惟一永恒的主题就是爱。

爱，尽管它的存在形式非常脆弱，却是惟一强大而持久的力量，

它给我们的日常生活带来了真正的意义。

The only theme that resonates throughout the numerous popular life theories is love.

Love, in all its fragile forms, is the one powerful, enduring force

that brings real meaning to our everyday lives.

当然，我不是在谈论罗曼蒂克、卿卿我我的爱，

尽管那本身也是一种相当强大的力量。

Of course, I'm not talking about romantic, "kissy-kissy" love,

although that is pretty powerful stuff in itself.

一颗破碎的心比伤口上撒盐更为痛苦，这已得到了广泛的证明。

It's well documented that a broken heart feels far more
painful than squeezing lemon juice over a deep paper cut.

但是，我所说的爱是在我们内心深处燃烧的火焰，是这种内心的温暖
使得心灵不会被令人绝望的冬天冰封。这是对生命本身的爱。

But the love I mean is the fire that burns inside us all, the inner warmth that prevents
our soul from freezing in the winters of despair. It's the love of life itself.

它是一种声音，在说："拥抱生命，尽情创造吧！"随之而来的是
对生命的激情和理解：生命中有些东西是值得为之赴汤蹈火的，
何况还有那么多值得为之活下去的东西。

It's the voice that says "Celebrate life, be creative!" It brings with it the
passion and understanding that some things in life are worth dying for,
but there is so much more worth living for.

它鼓励我们张开双臂迎接每一个时刻，就像在机场迎接一位故友，
它鼓励我们拥抱展现自我的机会，让我们为存在而感到快乐。

It encourages us to greet each moment the same way we greet an old friend
at the airport, to embrace opportunities to express
ourselves in a way that makes us feel glad we exist.

这种对生命的热爱引导我们帮助他人，
仅仅因为为周围的人做些事情感觉实在是太好了。

This love of life leads us to help others simply
because it feels great to contribute to those around us.

我们都知道，成为家人和朋友的可靠支柱是多么美好的感觉
（当然，也有局限）。

We all know how wonderful it feels to be a rock for our family and friends
(of course, there is a limit).

不过，尽管这听起来蛮不错的，"你来到世上就是为了过自己喜爱的生活"，
这好像也不错，可是仍然有一大堆纠缠不清的问题。

But as good as it sounds, and as much as "you're here to live the life you love"
rings true, it still brings up a whole pile of sticky questions.

特别是：你到底为什么来到这世上？你真正挚爱的是什么？

Specifically: Why exactly are you here?

What is it that you truly love?

那些不这样扪心自问的人总会满腹狐疑地审视生活，
不知道为什么生活没有更多的乐趣。

People who don't ask themselves these questions invariably go through life
wondering why it isn't a lot more fun.

他们经常感觉被遗弃了，

They often feel they've been left behind,

要么是他们说不清楚，但的确察觉到有些东西味道不对。

or they can't quite put it into words, but they sense

that something just smells a little funny.

其实，我们经常过于专注眼前的事情，而看不到前进的方向。

The truth is that often we're so focused on what we are doing
that we lose sight of where we are going.

但是，我们实际上在做什么呢？现代世界充满了令人质疑的
干扰、时限和次序。

But what are we actually doing? The modern world is filled
with questionable distractions, deadlines, and priorities.

昼夜混为一谈。

Day and night blur into one.

我们被接踵而至的恐惧和欲望包围，强迫我们加入一场不可能获胜的赛跑。

We get caught up in an avalanche of fears and desires

that propel us into a race we can't possibly win.

于是我们跑啊，跑啊，奔向生活中的一个理想目标，可然后怎么办呢？

So we rush, rush, rush to get to a certain

ideal point in our life, and then what?

就好像你开车一路狂奔到商店，赶快下车，然后竟然无法想起要买什么。

It's just like when you drive all the way to the store, get out of the car,

and then can't remember what you came for.

所以说，我们许多人一开始都梦想过一种无拘无束、自由驰骋的美好生活，

So many of us start off dreaming about a

wonderful life that is wild and free,

但通常我们实际到达的地方离企盼的目标还很远。

but that's usually a long way

from where we actually end up.

可悲的是，我们往往到最后才发现这个事实，但为时已晚。
你不可能再从头来过。
Sadly, we often discover this fact right at the end,
when it's too late. You can't start all over again.

让我告诉你吧，这个世界上有许多极其糟糕的感觉。

比如，"洗澡时水面冒泡"般的内疚，

And let me tell you, there are some awfully bad feelings

in this world. Like "bubbles in the bath" guilt,

"买鞋时发出难闻的脚臭"般的尴尬，

"pungent foot odor in the shoe store" embarrassment,

还有"我不敢相信第一次约会自己就做了那件事"般的焦虑。

and "I can't believe I did that
on the first date" anxiety.

但是在所有令你不快的糟糕感觉之中，最糟糕的莫过于明明知道曾
经有机会做真正喜爱的事，却没有抓住机会。

But of all the awful feelings that make you feel sick to your stomach, nothing feels
half as bad as knowing you had a chance to do what you truly love, and you didn't take it.

那么，你生活中的激情是什么呢？你被带到这个地球上，到底是为了什么？
这些问题的答案将解开生活的难解之谜，它就像问题来临时一样重大。

So what is your life's passion? What were you put on this earth to do?

The answer to these questions will unlock the great mystery of life;

it's as big as they come.

下面是几点启示，也许能帮助你开始有益的思考：

Here are a few hints that may help you get on the right track:

首先，没人会提醒你。这就像整天背着一块"踢我一脚"的招牌走来走去。
你必须自己发现问题。

First, no one is going to tell you about it. It's like walking around all day
with a sign on your back that says "Kick me." You must discover it for yourself.

同样，这样的事情也极不可能：突然有一天，你沐浴在明亮的阳光下，
你的生活目标神奇地展示在眼前。

It's also highly unlikely that one day you'll suddenly be bathed in
bright light and your life's purpose will be laid out in a divine vision,

而且，在电视上找到答案也纯属痴心妄想。
and it's guaranteed that you won't find it
on television.

是的，更为不可能的是：有一天，血液涌进你的大脑，
一切问题随之迎刃而解。

Yes, it's remotely possible that one day the blood will rush to your brain and

enable you to work it all out without too much bother,

但是，最好的办法是保证一些高质量的独处时间，好好想一想这些棘手的问题。

but the best way is to spend some quality time alone,

asking yourself the tough questions.

这做起来并不是那么困难，首先一定要诚实。

很简单："想从生活中得到更多的人请举手。"

This exercise is not that hard, and it's all about being honest.

It's as easy as "Raise your hand if you feel you could get more out of life."

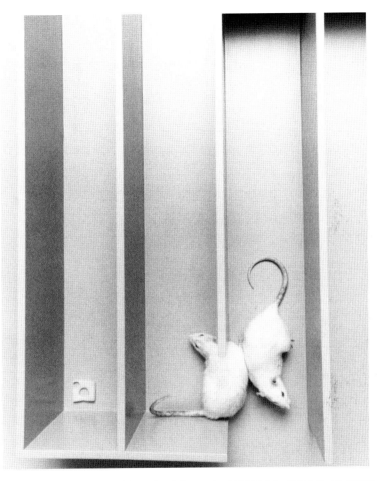

其次一定要关注最要紧的核心问题。不要管是谁动了你的奶酪，
先问问自己为什么要寻找奶酪！

It's also about getting to the essence of what really matters. Never mind who moved
your cheese—ask yourself why you were looking for cheese in the first place!

对一些人来说，这只不过是寻找生命中美丽而真实的时刻，
并围绕它们制定一个计划。

For some people this will simply be a case of seeking out the moments in
their life that are beautiful and true and then building a plan around them.

对另一些人而言，这好像朝深渊里看。

For others it may feel as if they are

staring into an abyss.

在极端情况下，这种强烈的内省会使大脑膨胀到危险的境地。
相信我，冒这种风险是值得的。

In extreme cases, such intense introspection may cause the brain to
swell to dangerous dimensions. Trust me, it's worth the risk.

如果你扪心自问这些重大问题，并倾听内心的回答，
你最终会听到命运的召唤。

If you ask the big questions and listen carefully to your
heart, you will eventually hear destiny call you.

如果你愿意倾听，一个微弱的声音——姑且称之为良知、
内在的自我或内心的岳母——总会告诉你真相。

A little voice—call it your conscience, your inner self, or your internal mother-in-
law—will always tell you the truth if you are prepared to hear it.

起初，你可能只觉得生活陷入了无法摆脱的惯例。

（嗨，大家欢迎你！）

At first you may only become aware of how your life has been stuck in a rut.

(Hey, join the club!)

然后，你可能意识到你真正想要的是什么，
但你就是不能让梦想成真。

Then you may realize what you really want,

but you just can't quite make it happen.

然而很快，你就会发现目标近在眼前。就好像你正在去海滩的途中，
却忽然想起家中的电熨斗插头还没拔。

Pretty soon, though, it will hit you right between the eyes. Just like when you're
halfway to the beach and suddenly remember that you left the iron on at home.

当你知道，或者仅仅怀疑自己知道，应该怎样生活的时候，就立即去做吧！
如果有必要，在黑暗中向前大胆地一跳，

And when you know, or even suspect you know, what you should be doing

with your life, then do it! Take a wild leap in the dark if you have to,

触地后马上奔跑，因为你必须争分夺秒。

then hit the ground running

because you don't have a second to lose.

尽管我们感觉自己不可战胜、长生不老，

In spite of our feelings of invincibility

and immortality,

但我们的生命远比想像的要脆弱。

our existence is far more tenuous

than we might think.

把手放在胸口，感受心脏的跳动。那其实就是你的生命之钟在滴答作响，细数着余下的时刻。有一天它会停止。这是千真万确的，而你对此绝对无能为力。

Place your hand over your chest and feel your heartbeat. That is actually your life clock ticking, counting down the moments you have left. One day it will stop. That is 100 percent guaranteed, and there's absolutely nothing you can do about it.

所以你不能浪费任何一秒钟珍贵的时光。精力充沛、满怀激情地追求梦想吧，
否则你只好止步不前，眼看着梦想付诸东流。

So you can't afford to throw away a single precious second. Go after your dreams with
energy and passion, or you may as well stand back and watch them wash down the drain.

如果你坐在栅栏上浪费生命，在余下的短暂时光中，你将最终一事无成。

（而且，当然，敏感区还会有扎刺儿的危险。）

If you waste your life sitting on the fence,

you'll end up going nowhere in the brief time you have left.

(And then, of course, there's a dangerous risk of splinters in delicate regions.)

正如人们所言，"你不可能两步就跨越鸿沟。"实现梦想需要勇气和付出。

As they say, "You can't cross a chasm in two small leaps."

It takes courage and commitment to live your dreams.

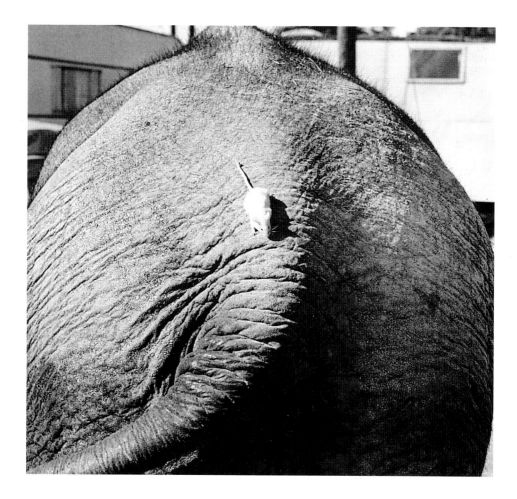

（当然，不要忘了勇气和愚蠢之间的界限。）

(Of course, one needs to remember where

courage ends and stupidity begins.)

事实上，我们所有人生来都拥有巨大的潜力，享有无数的机会，
可以达到令人眩晕的新高度。

The truth is, we are all born with potential greatness and blessed with
numerous opportunities to soar to dizzying new heights.

但可悲的是，我们许多人太懒惰，太在意别人的想法，或者太害怕变化，所以从未展开翅膀，展示我们巨大的天赋。

But sadly, many of us are too lazy, too concerned about what others might think, or too afraid of change to ever stretch our wings and realize our tremendous talents.

　　重要的是，做自己的事，做任何让你真正快乐的事，
而且要尽力做到最好。你所做的"事"并不重要，也许只不过是抟雪球，

It's so important that you just do your own thing—whatever makes you truly happy—
and do it as best you can. It doesn't matter whether your "thing" is making snowballs,

在水下憋气，

holding your breath underwater,

执著地叫喊，

hog calling,

或者手拿吹风机，创造出不同寻常的效果。惟一重要的是，
你对自己所做的事情感觉良好。

or wielding a hair-dryer with dramatic effect.

The only thing that matters is that you feel great about what you're doing.

记住，无论做什么，失误总是生活的一部分。

所以不要浪费时间，为过去追悔自责。

Keep in mind that whatever you do, mistakes are part of life.

So don't waste time kicking yourself for the past.

不要为自己的作为是否正确而思前想后、紧张不安。

你的内心总是知道答案的。

Don't stall or stress over whether you're doing the right thing.

You'll always know the answer in your heart.

不要感到沮丧，一定要记住，当你做非常重要而特殊的事情时，
总会遇到拒绝和抵触。

Rather than be discouraged, always remember that rejection and resistance are
almost guaranteed when you are doing something very important and very special.

当你决定追求梦想时，会有许多人（包括最爱你的人）竭力阻止你前进。

When you set out to live your dreams, lots of people (including those who love
you the most) will try to hold you back.

在这个世界上，有许多可怜的悲观主义者，他们放弃了梦想，
还告诉你："你在浪费时间——你永远不会成功的。"

In this world there are many miserable pessimists who have given up their dreams
and will tell you, "You're wasting your time—you'll never make it."

你的周围很可能会有这样一些人，他们内心里想让你的成就少一点，
甚至完全失败，这样他们自己就不会显得太难看。"算了吧，"
他们会说，"这不值得，而且本来对你也不合适。"

You may well be surrounded by people who secretly want you to achieve less or
even fail completely just so they don't look bad. "Forget about it," they'll say.
"It's not worth it and it's not right for you anyway."

所以重要的是要明白：坚持走自己的路非常值得，但绝非轻而易举。

So it's important to understand that following

your own path is incredibly rewarding,

but it's definitely not easy.

像每个人一样，有些日子会相对好过。

Like everyone else, you will have some days

that are better than others.

偶尔，一切都好像是一场灾难。

Occasionally, everything may seem like

a total disaster area.

当你告诉人们你想实现的目标时，人们可能会怪异地看着你，

People will look at you strangely when

you tell them what you are trying to achieve,

然后，你开始听信诋毁者的冷嘲热讽，开始怀疑自己：
"为什么，为什么我没有继续干卖热狗的工作？"
and you'll start to listen to your detractors
and doubt yourself. "Why, oh why, didn't I keep my job selling hot dogs?"

但是不管发生了什么事情，一定要坚持住！

But whatever happens, just hang on!

不要忘记，每个人都常常要奋力拼搏。

整天做着不喜欢或不关心的事情，真是让人精疲力竭。

Remember that everybody struggles at times. It's incredibly draining to live through the day doing something you really don't enjoy or even care about.

但是如果你追求梦想，你至少是为自己最爱干的事情而累趴下的。

But if you follow your dreams, at least you will exhaust
yourself doing what you love most.

现在，你也许认为这不符合事物的普遍发展规律。

但是相信我，这非常符合。

Now, you may not think that this will measure up to much in the
global scheme of things. But believe me, it does.

当你从生活中获得最大回报时，尽情品味最后一滴甘露，

When you get the most out of your life,

savoring every last drop,

它将改变你的一切，让你从平凡走向卓越。

it will transform everything about you

from ordinary to extraordinary.

如果做自己喜欢的事情，那么每天早上，掀开被子，

你会为新的一天的开始而激动不已，

When you do what you love, you can pull back the bed sheets every morning

feeling excited about beginning another day,

然后你会洋溢着真心的喜悦，并且感染他人。

and you'll be filled with a heartfelt joy

that is highly contagious.

就好像你开始放声大笑时，

Just like when you start laughing out loud,

也会引得别人大笑起来，

and you make someone else start laughing,

接着是另外一个人，

and then someone else,

直到你们都放声大笑，眼里含泪，肚子直痛，呼吸困难，甚至无法站立。

until you are all laughing so hard that your eyes water, you get

terrible stomach cramps, it's hard to breathe, and you can't even stand up.

然而最棒的是，做能使自己高兴得胡须卷起

（当然，假定你果真有胡须）的事情，

But best of all, by doing the things that make your whiskers curl up

with delight (assuming, of course, that you actually have whiskers),

你会激励他人也追逐梦想，

you will inspire someone else

to go after their dreams,

而这，我的朋友，就是你改变世界的方式！

and that, my friend,

is how you change the world!

你知道吗？即使你有重大失误，即使你几乎做错了所有事情，
你仍然会享受奇异无比、充满乐趣的生命旅程，

You know what? Even if you make big mistakes, if you're wrong about
almost everything, you'll still enjoy an amazing, fun-filled life adventure,

晚上睡觉时，你知道自己倾尽了全力，改变了生活，

you will go to sleep at night knowing you

gave your all and made a difference,

每天醒来时，你期盼着一个最美丽、最激动的未来。

and wake up each day looking forward to a future that is

as beautiful and exciting as you can imagine.

还有，你知道吗？只要你聆听自己的心，开动脑筋，

You know something else? If you just listen

to your heart and use you're head,

那你永远都不会错的。

you'll never be wrong.